SCIENCE BEHIND THE COLORS
SEA SLUGS

by Alicia Z. Klepeis

pogo

Ideas for Parents and Teachers

Pogo Books let children practice reading informational text while introducing them to nonfiction features such as headings, labels, sidebars, maps, and diagrams, as well as a table of contents, glossary, and index.

Carefully leveled text with a strong photo match offers early fluent readers the support they need to succeed.

Before Reading

- "Walk" through the book and point out the various nonfiction features. Ask the student what purpose each feature serves.
- Look at the glossary together. Read and discuss the words.

Read the Book

- Have the child read the book independently.
- Invite him or her to list questions that arise from reading.

After Reading

- Discuss the child's questions. Talk about how he or she might find answers to those questions.
- Prompt the child to think more. Ask: Sea slugs can change color to camouflage themselves. Do you know any other creatures that do this?

Pogo Books are published by Jump!
5357 Penn Avenue South
Minneapolis, MN 55419
www.jumplibrary.com

Library of Congress Cataloging-in-Publication Data

Names: Klepeis, Alicia, 1971- author.
Title: Sea slugs / by Alicia Z. Klepeis.
Description: Pogo books edition.
Minneapolis, MN: Jump!, Inc, 2021.
Series: Science behind the colors | Includes index.
Audience: Ages 7-10 | Audience: Grades 2-3
Identifiers: LCCN 2019057312 (print)
LCCN 2019057313 (ebook)
ISBN 9781645275893 (hardcover)
ISBN 9781645275909 (paperback)
ISBN 9781645275916 (ebook)
Subjects: LCSH: Nudibranchia—Juvenile literature.
Classification: LCC QL430.4 .K59 2021 (print)
LCC QL430.4 (ebook) | DDC 594/.36—dc23
LC record available at https://lccn.loc.gov/2019057312
LC ebook record available at https://lccn.loc.gov/2019057313

Editor: Jenna Gleisner
Designer: Molly Ballanger

Photo Credits: Matt_Potenski/iStock, cover; Levent Konuk/Shutterstock, 1, 3; Douglas Klug/Getty, 4; Brook Peterson/Stocktrek Images/Getty, 5; Sahara Frost/Shutterstock, 6-7; Jaime Franch Wildlife Photo/Alamy, 8-9; John Wall/Alamy, 10; Bass Supakit/Shutterstock, 11; Andrey_Kuzmin/Shutterstock, 12-13 (background); Paul Starosta/Getty, 12-13 (top); Magnus Lundgren/Wild Wonders of China/Nature Picture Library, 12-13 (bottom); zaferkizilkaya/Shutterstock, 14-15; Johannes Kornelius/Shutterstock, 16 (top); cynoclub/Shutterstock, 16 (bottom); RibeirodosSantos/iStock, 17; Tidewater Teddy/Shutterstock, 18-19; Tobias Friedrich/F1 ONLINE/SuperStock, 20-21; cbpix/Shutterstock, 23.

Printed in the United States of America at Corporate Graphics in North Mankato, Minnesota.

TABLE OF CONTENTS

CHAPTER 1

AS SLOW AS SLUGS

What ocean creature comes in every color of the rainbow? What has no legs or backbone? This multicolored **mollusk** is a sea slug!

There are more than 3,000 **species** of sea slugs! More are discovered each year. They come in different shapes and colors. This one is called the sea bunny! Can you see why?

Sea slugs live in oceans all around the world. They can be shorter than your fingernail or longer than a ruler! All are **invertebrates**. They have soft bodies. Some can swim, but others cannot.

DID YOU KNOW?

The sea slug's official name is nudibranch. We also call them sea slugs. Why? They move slowly. They often slide along the ocean floor on their bellies. As they move, they leave trails of slime behind. Ew!

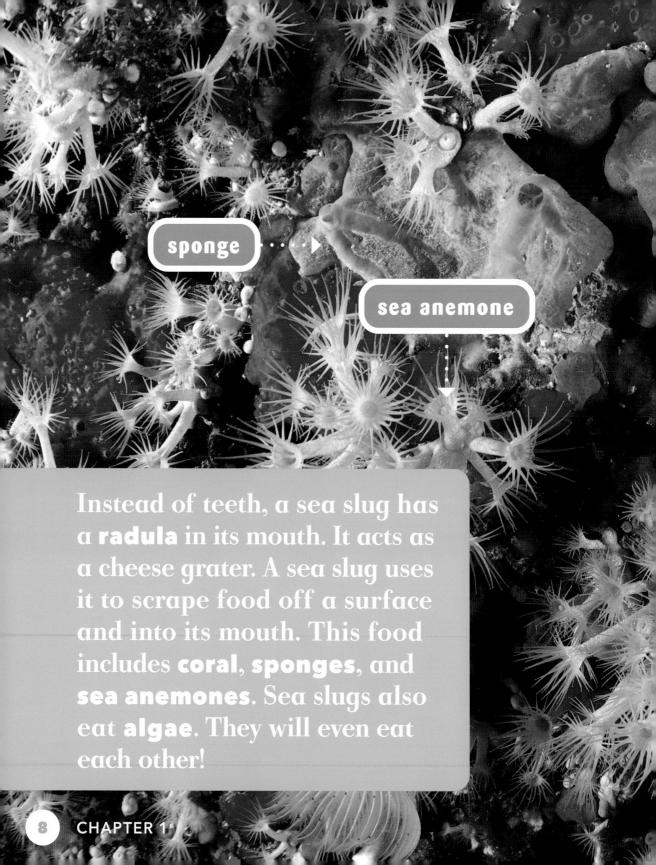

sponge ·····▶

sea anemone

Instead of teeth, a sea slug has a **radula** in its mouth. It acts as a cheese grater. A sea slug uses it to scrape food off a surface and into its mouth. This food includes **coral**, **sponges**, and **sea anemones**. Sea slugs also eat **algae**. They will even eat each other!

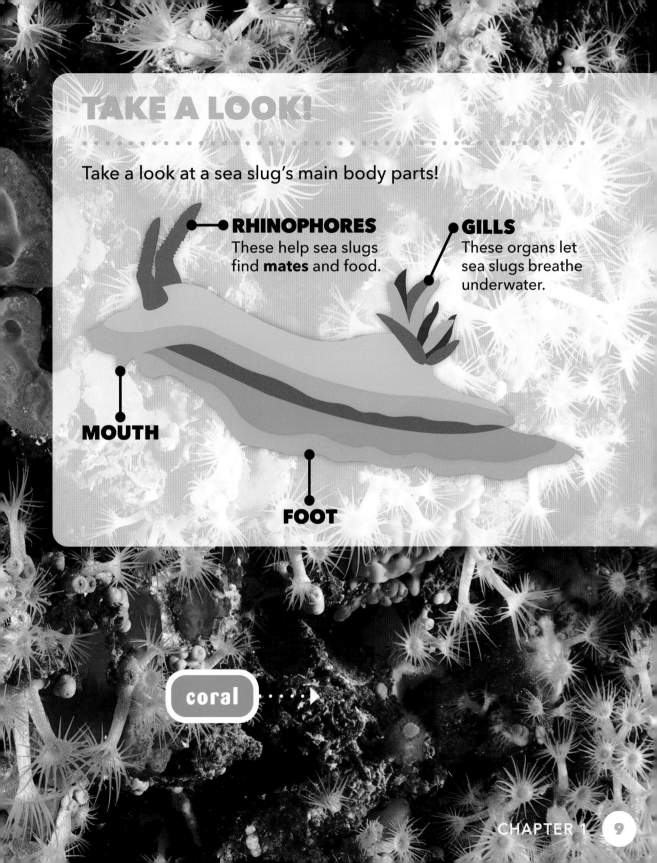

TAKE A LOOK!

Take a look at a sea slug's main body parts!

RHINOPHORES
These help sea slugs find **mates** and food.

GILLS
These organs let sea slugs breathe underwater.

MOUTH

FOOT

coral ••••▶

CHAPTER 2

CRAZY COLORS

How do sea slugs get their colors? It depends. Some get their colors from the **prey** they eat. The Hopkins' rose sea slug is one. It is bright pink. Why? It eats pink sea creatures.

Hopkins' rose sea slug

This one is bright green.
Why? It eats green algae!

adult Spanish dancer

young Spanish dancer

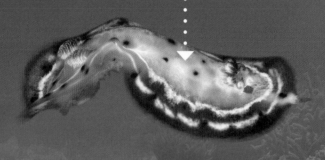

Sometimes their **genes** determine their color. In these cases, sea slugs grow into their colors when they are adults. Spanish dancer sea slugs are one example.

TAKE A LOOK!

Sea slugs have a unique life cycle. Take a look at the **stages**!

LARVA

Larvae hatch from eggs. They swim and have a shell for protection.

JUVENILE

At this stage, the sea slug sheds its shell.

ADULT

Sea slug adults are fully grown. They are able to lay eggs.

Sea slugs are colorblind. What does this mean? They can't recognize certain colors or sometimes any color at all. Their eyes likely see only dark and light. So they can't appreciate their own coloring!

Because they can't see well, they use their sense of smell to guide them. This helps them find food and mates.

CHAPTER 3
HIDING AND WARNING COLORS

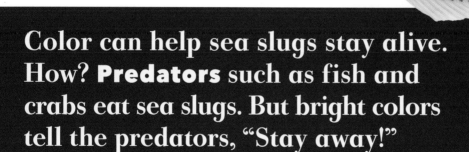

Color can help sea slugs stay alive. How? **Predators** such as fish and crabs eat sea slugs. But bright colors tell the predators, "Stay away!"

The food that sea slugs eat can change more than their color. It can also make them poisonous to predators.

Some sea slugs look like their surroundings. This **camouflage** hides them from predators.

They can also look like their prey. How? They get color from the food they eat. So when a sea slug feeds on a sponge, it blends in with it.

Sea slugs only live about one year. Their lives are short, but their colors stand out! Would you like to see a sea slug?

DID YOU KNOW?

Sea slugs are not very active. Some spend almost their entire lives on the same sponge or coral reef.

ACTIVITIES & TOOLS

TRY THIS!

HIDE-AND-SEEK SEA SLUGS

Some sea slugs blend in with their surroundings. See how camouflage works with this activity!

What You Need:

- scissors
- colored paper (four different colors)
- newspaper
- plastic food storage bag
- glue or tape
- stopwatch
- pencil
- notebook

1. Cut out one fish shape from each color paper.

2. Cut out four fish shapes from the newspaper.

3. Cut out four fish shapes from the plastic food storage bag.

4. Glue or tape each of the fish onto a large piece of newspaper.

5. Set your stopwatch for 30 seconds. Have a friend, sibling, or parent try to find as many fish as they can during this time.

6. How many fish did they find? Which ones did they find first? Which ones took the longest to find? Record the results in your notebook.

GLOSSARY

algae: Small plants without roots or stems that grow mainly in water.

camouflage: An animal's natural form or coloring that allows it to blend in with its surroundings.

coral: A sea creature known as a polyp that lives in a colony and forms a hard skeleton that becomes part of a reef.

genes: Parts of living things that are passed from parents to offspring and determine how one looks and grows.

invertebrates: Animals that do not have backbones.

larvae: The very early forms of an animal after hatching.

mates: The breeding partners of a pair of animals.

mollusk: An invertebrate animal that has a soft body without segments.

predators: Animals that hunt other animals for food.

prey: Animals that are hunted by other animals for food.

radula: A rough band of teeth, found in some mollusks, that can scrape food and take it into its mouth.

sea anemones: Invertebrate sea animals that look like flowers and have tentacles around their mouths.

species: One of the groups into which similar animals and plants are divided.

sponges: Sea animals that have rubbery skeletons with many holes.

stages: Steps or periods of development.

INDEX

TO LEARN MORE

Finding more information is as easy as 1, 2, 3.

1. Go to www.factsurfer.com
2. Enter "seaslugs" into the search box.
3. Click the "Surf" button to see a list of websites.

FACT SURFER